Teasing Isn't Funny

What to Do About Emotional Bullying

by Melissa Higgins

pictures by Simone Shin

PICTURE WINDOW BOOKS
a capstone imprint

Note to Parents and Educators

Bullying is a serious problem that many children experience. Emotional bullying can include taunting, humiliation, excluding, and repeated, hurtful teasing in the presence of others. Bullying can cause the bullied child to feel depressed or ashamed. It can lower a child's self esteem and academic performance. Kids and adults must learn to recognize bullying behavior and develop immediate and fair ways to stop it.

This book is intended for an adult to read with a child. While reading, encourage the child to volunteer his or her own experiences about a time when he or she was emotionally bullied, acted as a bully, or saw emotional bullying taking place. Use the text and illustrations as a jumping-off point for conversation and problem solving. For example, what does the child think about the advice Alex gives Kelly? Who would the child feel comfortable talking to if he or she was bullied? What other ideas does the child have for dealing with someone who uses emotional bullying?

Thanks to our adviser for her expertise, research, and advice:
Dorothy L. Espelage, PhD
Department of Educational Psychology
University of Illinois, Urbana-Champaign

Editor: Michelle Hasselius
Designer: Lori Bye
Creative Director: Nathan Gassman
Production Specialist: Laura Manthe
The illustrations in this book were created digitally.

Picture Window Books are published by Capstone,
1710 Roe Crest Drive, North Mankato, Minnesota 56003
www.capstonepub.com

Design elements: Shutterstock:JungleOutThere

Library of Congress Cataloging-in-Publication Data
Higgins, Melissa, 1953–
Teasing isn't funny : what to do about emotional bullying / by Melissa Higgins.
pages cm. — (Picture window books. No more bullies)
Audience: K to Grade 3.
Summary: "Sensitive, narrative text from illustrated animal characters shows readers what emotional bullying is and provides possible solutions to stop it"—Provided by publisher.
ISBN 978-1-4795-6940-3 (library binding)
ISBN 978-1-4795-6956-4 (paperback)
ISBN 978-1-4795-6960-1 (eBook PDF)
1. Teasing—Juvenile literature. 2. Bullying—Juvenile literature. 3. Bullying—Prevention—Juvenile literature. I. Title.
BF637.T43H54 2016
302.34'3—dc23   2014049227

Printed in the United States of America
in North Mankato, Minnesota.
032015   008823CGF15

It's cold waiting for the school bus. I pull my jacket snug.

Someone snickers behind me. Then I hear whispers.

My stomach turns. I wish the bus would hurry up and get here.

"Ew, yuck. Did a mouse sleep on Kelly's head last night?"

I don't have to turn to see who's talking about me.
It's Sam. It's always Sam.

Sam's friend, Jesse, laughs. **"Kelly's mom is so
poor, she can't buy Kelly a comb. How sad."**

Something scratches my wrist. I look down.
It's a dirty plastic comb. They probably found
it in the gutter.

"Take it," Sam says. **"I have a ton at home."**

I shake my head. I wish they'd leave me alone.

Sometimes teasing can be fun and playful. But if someone's teasing makes you feel bad about yourself, that's emotional bullying. Emotional bullying can also include taunting, humiliation, spreading rumors, and ganging up on others.

"Go on! Take it!" Sam slides the dirty comb into my pocket.

I don't know what to do. Everyone is watching.

"You could say thank you," Sam says.

"Poor people have bad manners," says Jesse. "They're ugly too."

I feel like a bug. A tiny, awful bug.

The bus pulls up, and I step closer to the curb.
The door opens. Sam and Jesse push ahead of me.

"Beauty before ugly," Jesse says loudly.

I climb on behind them. They trot to the back seat. The only open seats are near them. I take a deep breath and sit next to Erin. Erin slides away from me, closer to the window.

It's like I have a disease no one wants to catch.

Things are quiet for a while. My shoulders drop a little. Maybe it will be OK now.

Then Sam yells, **"Who's the ugliest kid at school?"**

About 1 in 3 students says he or she is bullied during the school year.

Jesse chants, **"Ug-ly! Kel-ly!"**

A few other kids join in. **"Ug-ly! Kel-ly!"**

My face burns. I want to disappear.

The bus finally gets to school. I climb off as fast as I can.

Someone walks next to me. Oh no. Now what?

"Kelly?"

I look over. It's Alex. Alex is in my class.

11

"Hi," Alex says. "I just want to say it's not right how those kids treat you. It's mean. And you're not ugly. I hope you don't believe them."

I didn't know anyone cared. I push back tears. **"Thanks."**

"Have you told anyone?" Alex asks. "Like your parents or Mr. West?"

Mr. West is our teacher. I shake my head no. Sam and Jesse are really popular. I'm too ashamed to tell anyone what they say about me.

"Well," Alex says, "it's just an idea. But I'm sure an adult can help if you say something." Alex smiles.

A simple way to help someone who's being bullied is to make him or her feel included. Say hi in the hallway, or sit with him or her at lunch.

13

Alex seems to understand what I'm going through.
All day I think about what Alex said. Sam and Jesse
are mean. I'm *not* ugly. It's *not* right.

After recess, I pass the principal, Ms. Mills, in the hallway.
I like Ms. Mills. She's friendly to everyone.

"Hello, Kelly," she says. "How are you?"

I stop in front of her.

"Kelly?" she asks. "Is something wrong?"

I nod. "Can I talk to you?"

Ms. Mills takes me to her office. **"Tell me what's bothering you."**

I tell her that kids are mean to me, especially on the bus.

"In what way are they mean?" she asks.

It's hard to tell her, but I do. I hope she believes me.

"I'm sorry this is happening to you, Kelly," she says. **"And I'm glad you told me. You're being bullied. We don't allow bullying at our school, not even on the school bus."** Ms. Mills says she'll talk to Sam and Jesse, and the bus driver.

That scares me. **"They'll think I tattled,"** I say. **"It will make things worse."**

"You leave that to me," Ms. Mills says with a reassuring smile. **"In the meantime, do you have a friend on the bus you can sit with?"**

"No," I answer. Then I think about Alex. **"Well, maybe."**

After school I see Alex heading for our bus. I run and catch up.

"I talked to Ms. Mills," I say.

"Great!" Alex says. **"I bet you feel better."**

I think about it. I *do* feel better. It's like my shoulders aren't so heavy.

Kids who have at least one friend are less likely to be bullied than kids without any friends.

19

We board the bus. I hear Sam and Jesse laughing in the back seat.

"Alex?" I ask. "Is it OK if I sit with you?"

"As long as you don't mind sitting in front," Alex says. "I used to get teased a lot. Staying near the bus driver helps."

Alex and I talk on the ride home. I tell Alex about my hamster, Gus. Alex walks dogs at an animal shelter. It sounds like fun. **"You can come with me sometime,"** Alex says. **"They always need volunteers."**

Doing a fun activity outside of school, such as a sport, club, or volunteering, is a great way to make friends and feel better about yourself.

The bus arrives at my stop. I get an idea.

"Hey, Alex?" I ask. "Do you want to sit together on the bus in the morning?"

"Sure," Alex says with a wave. "See you tomorrow."

"Great! See you tomorrow." I wave back.

If Sam and Jesse have been talking about me, I don't hear them. And I don't care. I made a new friend today.

Glossary

ashamed—to feel shame, guilt, or embarrassment

bully—to frighten or pick on someone over and over

emotional—to have or show strong feelings

humiliate—to make someone look or feel foolish or embarrassed

rumor—something said by many people; a rumor may not be true

taunt—to try to make someone angry or upset by teasing him or her

tease—to make fun of someone; teasing can be hurtful or playful, depending on how it makes the other person feel

volunteer—to do a job, usually without pay

Read More

Cook, Julia. *Tease Monster: A Book About Teasing vs. Bullying.* Building Relationships. Boys Town, Neb.: Boys Town Press, 2013.

Hall, Pamela. *Making a Bully-Free World. A Bully-Free World.* Minneapolis: Magic Wagon, 2013.

Manushkin, Fran. *No More Teasing.* Katie Woo. Minneapolis: Picture Window Books, 2010.

Internet Sites

FactHound offers a safe, fun way to find Internet sites related to this book. All of the sites on FactHound have been researched by our staff.

Here's all you do:

Visit *www.facthound.com*

Type in this code: 9781479569403

Super-cool stuff!

Check out projects, games and lots more at
www.capstonekids.com

Index

All of the books in the series: